# THE ADVENTURES OF ARI STINKY SMELLY & SNIFFY

The Guardian Resurrection Day of Pascha

ISBN: 978-1-7644581-4-6



To request access to the archives of magic or to whisper a message across dimensions: B3STOW ™ KREA PREA ™ Est.2012

*The word **Pascha** is ancient it comes from the Hebrew **Pesach**, meaning "Passover," and travelled through Aramaic and Greek before reaching the world as a symbol of renewal and light. In this story, Pascha is not just a tradition; it's a bridge between cultures, a reminder that Resurrection rebirth and hope belong to everyone. May this tale bring warmth, laughter, and the light of Pascha to all who read it.*

*Panagiota Makaronis*

It was Holy Thursday morning, the beginning of the most special days of Greek Orthodox Easter. Ari woke up early in his little bed, the room still soft and quiet. Something warm fluttered in his chest like a dream he couldn't quite remember, but it felt important, like a secret waiting to unfold. When Ari heard his mum's voice ring out from the kitchen, warm and commanding in that way only mums can manage. "Time to get up properly now, Ari! Breakfast is ready. Get dressed and brush your teeth!"

Ari dribbled his little basketball across the lounge room floor, the thump-thump echoing through the quiet autumn morning. His messy brown hair bounced as he leapt toward the toy hoop on the wall, the black-and-white puppy yapping excitedly while the ginger kitten chased the ball's shadow. Just as Ari lined up another shot, his mum's voice called from the kitchen, warm and firm: "Time to go, Ari! we're going for a run to the park!" Ari's eyes lit up instantly. A run to the park on Holy Thursday felt like the perfect start to the day, and he dashed toward his room, already imagining the cool air and the crunch of fallen leaves under his shoes.

From the kitchen, Betty watched with a soft smile, sipping her coffee as the morning light glowed across her emerald-green jacket. Holy Thursday had begun quietly, but in their home, it already felt full of life, warmth, and the promise of something magical stirring in the air.

Ari zoomed along the autumn path on his blue scooter, leaves swirling around his wheels like tiny dancers. His puppy sprinted beside him, ears flapping, trying its best to keep up. Betty jogged just behind, her emerald-green jacket bright against the golden trees, calling out with a laugh, "Slow down just a little, Ari! I can't catch you!" Ari giggled, pushing faster, the cool breeze brushing his cheeks as ducks glided across the lake nearby. The whole morning felt alive crisp air, crunching leaves, and the warm feeling of being together on Holy Thursday.

Ari sped along the lakeside path on his scooter, his blue-and-yellow helmet shining under the soft autumn sun. The three teddy bears peeking from his backpack bounced with every push, and his little puppy raced ahead, barking as if cheering him on. Betty jogged behind him, laughing as she called out, "Not too fast, Ari! I still need to catch you!" Ari turned his head just enough to shout back, "Come on, Mum! You can do it!" before zooming forward again, leaves swirling around his wheels while ducks glided calmly across the water beside them and the whole morning felt like a happy adventure made just for them.

Ari zipped along the path on his scooter, laughing as the orange kitten Uri darted in front of him and the little black-and-white puppy Pouey bounded after them both. "Hey! Wait for me!" Betty called out between breaths, jogging behind him with a smile that matched the golden autumn trees. Ari turned his head just enough to shout back, "Come on, Mum! You're too slow!" before pushing off again, leaves swirling around his wheels while ducks glided across the lake beside them. The whole morning felt like a happy race no one really wanted to win.

Ari tip-toed toward the café tables, gripping his scooter with one hand and trying not to giggle. "Mummy, look! It's Aunty Melanie and Yia-Yia Dimi!" he whispered, eyes sparkling with mischief. Aunty Melanie was busy scrolling on her phone, completely unaware, while Yia-Yia Dimi calmly read her newspaper under the big red umbrella. Ari leaned closer to Betty and whispered, "Let's sneak up on them and scare them!" Betty covered her smile with her hand and whispered back, "Alright… but quietly, little ninja." Ari nodded, puffed up with excitement, as the puppy and kitten bounced around him, ready to join the surprise attack.

Ari crouched low behind his scooter, eyes sparkling with mischief as he whispered, "Okay, Mummy… I'm gonna do it now!" The puppy wiggled with excitement, the kitten's tail flicked like a tiny orange flag, and Betty tried not to laugh as she nodded. Ari took a deep breath, then jumped out from behind the table with a loud, "BOO!" Aunty Melanie nearly dropped her phone, gasping before bursting into laughter, and Yia-Yia Dimi clutched her chest dramatically. "Ay, Panagia mou, Ari!" she exclaimed, then smiled wide. "You scared us good, koukla mou!" The whole table erupted in giggles, the moment warm and full of family joy under the red umbrella.

Ari settled into his chair at the café table, still glowing with pride from his perfectly executed "BOO!" as everyone gathered around him. Yia-Yia Dimi folded her newspaper and shook her head with a smile. "You little troublemaker, you nearly scared the soul out of me," she teased, reaching over to pinch his cheek. Aunty Melanie laughed, putting her phone down. "Ari, you're too quick for us! I didn't even see you coming." Betty wrapped her hands around her warm cup and leaned back, watching her family with that soft, grateful smile she saved for moments like this. The puppy and kitten curled up under the table, tails flicking, while autumn leaves drifted around them. Ari looked from face to face and said proudly, "I got you all good, didn't I?" and the whole table burst into laughter, the morning feeling full and happy.

It was late on Holy Thursday morning when they all piled into the car, the air buzzing with that special Easter-week excitement. Yia-Yia Dimi took the wheel, steady and confident, while Betty sat in the front seat, turning around every so often to smile at Ari. In the back, Aunty Melanie buckled herself in beside him, and Ari could barely sit still. “We’re going to see Papou Costa, right? And then the poultry farm? And we’re buying eggs to dye them red, yeah?” he asked in one long breath, his eyes shining. Melanie laughed. “Yes, Ari, all of that!” Ari kicked his little feet happily. “This is the best Holy Thursday ever!” he declared, as the car rolled down the road toward Kalkallo, the trees flashing past like they were cheering them on.

Ari pressed his face to the window, eyes wide as the landscape opened into rolling paddocks dotted with animals. "Mummy, look! That bird looks like a pterodactyl!" he shouted, pointing at the tall white bird gliding over the fields. The whole car burst into laughter Ari was deep in his dinosaur era, and everything reminded him of a creature from the past. As they drove on, he bounced in his seat, naming every animal he saw. "Horses! Cows! Chickens! Goats!" he called out, each sighting more exciting than the last. The drive to Kalkallo felt like its own little adventure, the kind that made Holy Thursday morning feel magical.

As they pulled into the poultry farm, the car slowed and Ari's eyes grew huge. Right there by the fence stood a magnificent black stallion, its coat shining like polished midnight in the autumn sun. "Mummy, look! A real stallion!" Ari gasped, pressing his hands to the window. Yia-Yia Dimi parked the car, smiling as the horse lifted its head proudly, as if welcoming them. Aunty Melanie rested a gentle hand on Ari's shoulder while they leaned forward to get a better look. The moment felt still and special, the kind of surprise that makes a simple Holy Thursday outing feel magical.

Ari stepped up to the fence with his mum right beside him, his small hand slipping into hers as the black stallion lowered its head. The horse's warm breath puffed softly against Ari's fingers, and he let out a tiny gasp. "Mummy… he's so big," he whispered, half-in awe, half-in delight. Betty smiled, resting her hand gently on his back. "Go on, Agapi mou, give him a pat. He's saying hello." Ari reached out, brushing his hand over the stallion's smooth, dark nose, and the horse blinked slowly, calm and gentle. For a moment, everything felt still the hills, the breeze, even the chatter from the poultry farm just Ari, his mum, and the beautiful stallion sharing a quiet Holy Thursday moment.

Ari crouched down the moment they finished buying the eggs, completely mesmerised by the chickens wandering around the yard. One fluffy hen strutted a little closer, pecking gently at the ground, and Ari's whole face lit up. "Mummy, can I pat this one?" he whispered, already reaching out with careful fingers. Betty smiled and nodded, watching him move slowly so he wouldn't scare it. The hen paused, blinked up at him, and let Ari gently stroke its soft feathers. "She's so cute," he said, his voice full of wonder, while Yia-Yia Dimi and Aunty Melanie looked on proudly, the morning feeling warm and full of simple magic.

Ari hugged his teddy a little closer as the car turned down the quiet country road, on that late-morning drive, sun glowing warm across the fields. The sign for the cemetery appeared ahead, and he pressed his face to the window, watching the gates come into view. The chatter from the poultry farm faded into a soft silence, replaced by a gentle calm that settled over everyone in the car. "We're nearly there, Mummy," Ari said softly, his voice full of that sweet mix of excitement and respect. Betty turned in her seat and smiled at him, and Yia-Yia Dimi slowed the car as they approached the entrance. Aunty Melanie reached over and squeezed Ari's hand. "Papou Costa will be happy we came," she said, and Ari nodded, ready to visit him with all the love he carried.

Ari stood quietly between Betty and Yia-Yia Dimi, looking at the flowers they had placed, the photo on the stone, the name he had heard so many times. He never met his Papou, but something in him always felt connected, like a thread tied gently from his little heart to the man he'd never seen or met. He held his teddy close and whispered, "Hi, Papou… it's me, Ari." Betty watched him with a soft ache in her chest; she had always believed that Ari carried a piece of her father's spirit, the same warmth in his eyes, the same gentle curiosity. The breeze moved through the trees as if acknowledging them, and Ari looked up and said, "Mummy… I think Papou knows we're here." It felt true in a way that didn't need explaining just a quiet, sacred knowing.

As they drove out of Kalkallo Cemetery that, the late-afternoon light soft on the headstones, Ari paused and looked over his shoulder one more time at Papou Costa's grave. Betty and Yia-Yia Dimi were still sharing gentle stories. How Papou Costa & Yia-Yia Dimi owned a Poultry Farm for a while. How he used to whistle while he worked, and how he had two Dogs, Spiro the Kelpie and Max the Short Haired Pointer. He loved working on the farm. He loved Driving the Tractor Feeding the Animals how he always brought home treats, how he laughed with his whole chest.

Ari listened quietly, holding his three teddy bears tight against him. "I wish I could've met him," he said softly, his voice small but steady. Then he added, almost like a secret meant for the wind, "But I think he knows me anyway." Yia-Yia Dimi's eyes glistened as she nodded. "He does, Ari mou. He's with you every day." Ari smiled at that one of those deep, knowing smiles and whispered, "Bye, Papou. I'll come back again," While Ari sat in the car, with a heart full of love and something that felt a lot like connection.

Ari stood on his tiptoes at Yia-Yia's kitchen table, the whole room glowing with that warm Holy Thursday feeling as bowls, towels, and eggs covered the surface. Yia-Yia Dimi guided his little hand gently into the bowl of deep red dye, smiling as the colour slowly wrapped around the egg. Betty and Aunty Melanie watched proudly, each holding an egg of their own, the air filled with laughter, stories, and the soft scent of candles burning nearby. Ari's eyes sparkled as he lifted the egg out of the dye. "Look, Yia-Yia! It's so red!" he said, amazed. "Kokkino, Agapi mou," she replied, kissing the top of his head. "Just like we've always done." The moment felt like tradition, love, and family all woven together in one perfect afternoon.

The kitchen filled with the soft rhythm of hands working dough, the air warm with flour, tradition, and the quiet comfort of being together. It was still Holy Thursday, and after dyeing the eggs, everyone gathered around Yia-Yia's wooden table to make koulourakia. Ari stood between Betty and Yia-Yia Dimi, his little fingers trying to twist the dough into perfect braids just like hers. "Like this, koukla mou," she said, guiding his hands with her own, her touch gentle and sure. Aunty Melanie laughed as one of Ari's twists came out lopsided but full of charm. "That one's Papou Costa's," Ari declared proudly, placing it on the tray. The room glowed with golden afternoon light, icons watching over them from the shelf, and for a moment it felt like all the generations, past and present, were gathered in that kitchen, shaping dough and memory together.

Ari lay back against his pillow, still buzzing from the long, beautiful Holy Thursday, when Betty gently brushed his hair from his forehead. The room felt soft and safe, the kind of quiet that comes after a day full of family, tradition, and love. “Tomorrow is Good Friday, Ari,” she said softly. “We’re going to the Epitaphio.” Ari’s eyes widened with excitement. “I know! I’m not scared anymore,” he said proudly, hugging Stinky, Smelly, and Sniffy closer. “When I was little, the icons made me cry… but I’m a big boy now. I won’t cry in church.” Betty smiled, her heart full. “You are a big boy. And Papou Costa will be proud of you.” Ari nodded, already imagining the candles, the procession, the night air filled with incense and hymns. “I’m gonna be brave,” he whispered, drifting toward sleep, wrapped in tradition and the feeling of growing up just a little more.

The sun hung low over Kalkallo as the family gathered at Papou Costa's tombstone, the air thick with reverence and memory. Yia-Yia Dimi stood quietly, her eyes resting on the photo etched into the stone, while her eldest daughter Melanie placed a gentle hand on her arm. Nicholas, the middle son, stood behind them, his hand resting protectively on Yia-Yia's shoulder, grounding her with quiet strength. Betty stood beside Ari, as he looked up at the grave with wide, thoughtful eyes. "We're going to church soon, Papou," he whispered. "It's Good Friday." The flowers rustled softly in the breeze, and for a moment, it felt like Papou Costa was there with them woven into the fabric of their love, their tradition, and the sacred night ahead.

There Ari stood, with his family at the church on Good Friday, the air thick with incense and candlelight, gathered around the Epitaphio. A sacred symbol of Christ's burial. Draped in flowers and reverence, the Epitaphio represents the tomb of Jesus, carried in solemn procession to mark His death and the hope of resurrection. As the faithful kissed the icon and crawled beneath it, they weren't just honouring tradition, they were participating in a ritual of humility, grief, and deep spiritual connection. For Ari, it was his first time not crying, his heart brave and open, sensing that this wasn't just ceremony it was love, memory, and the mystery of something greater.

As they stood outside the church, candles glowing softly in their hands, the night felt sacred in a way Ari could finally understand. The Epitaphio shimmered with flowers and candlelight, and the crowd around them moved with a quiet, shared reverence. For Ari, this moment was not only sacred but huge his first Good Friday where he wasn't afraid, where the icons didn't overwhelm him, where he felt brave enough to stand tall beside his family. He felt the weight of the tradition, but also the warmth of it, like he was part of something ancient and beautiful. For the family, and for every person gathered there, the procession meant honouring Christ's journey to the tomb, walking with humility, grief, and hope. It was a reminder of love, sacrifice, and the promise of resurrection. But for Ari, it was also a step into growing up understanding his culture, his faith, and the legacy of the people who came before him. He held his candle steady, proud and calm, knowing Papou Costa would be smiling at how far he'd come.

Its Easter Saturday, and as midnight approached, the church grew darker and quieter, everyone waiting for that one sacred moment. Ari held his candle close, standing between his mum and Yia-Yia Dimi, feeling the same mix of excitement and mystery that filled the whole crowd. And then right at 12 a.m., Easter Sundaythe priest stepped out with the Holy Light, and the darkness broke. One flame became two, then ten, then a hundred, until the entire church glowed like a living sunrise.

***"Christos Anesti." "Christ is Risen."***

This moment happens at midnight because it marks the exact turning point from death to life, from sorrow to resurrection. It is the first breath of Easter, the moment Christ is proclaimed risen, and the world is symbolically reborn. For Ari, watching the flame reach him felt like being part of something ancient and powerful. For the family, it was a reminder of every generation before them who had stood in that same light. And as Ari's candle touched his mother's and the flame passed to him, he felt it hope, courage, and the quiet pride of growing up within a tradition that loved him long before he was born.

After forty days of fasting, discipline, and waiting, the moment finally arrived. It was just after midnight Easter Sunday had begun and the whole family gathered around Yia-Yia Dimi's table, the room glowing with warmth and relief. The pot of magiritsa sat in the centre, steaming gently as Yia-Yia served everyone their first spoonful. This soup wasn't just a meal; it was the traditional way to break the long Lenten fast. Magiritsa is light, warm, and easy on the stomach, easing the body back into eating after weeks of simplicity. But more than that, it symbolises new life, renewal, and the joy of the Resurrection. Beside the soup, a bowl of bright red eggs waited to be cracked, each one dyed the colour of life and Christ's sacrifice. Ari sat proudly at the table, his candle still glowing faintly beside him, feeling the magic of the moment. For Yia-Yia Dimi, it was the joy of seeing her family continue the rituals she had carried her whole life. And for everyone gathered, it was the perfect beginning to Easter together, grateful, and filled with light.

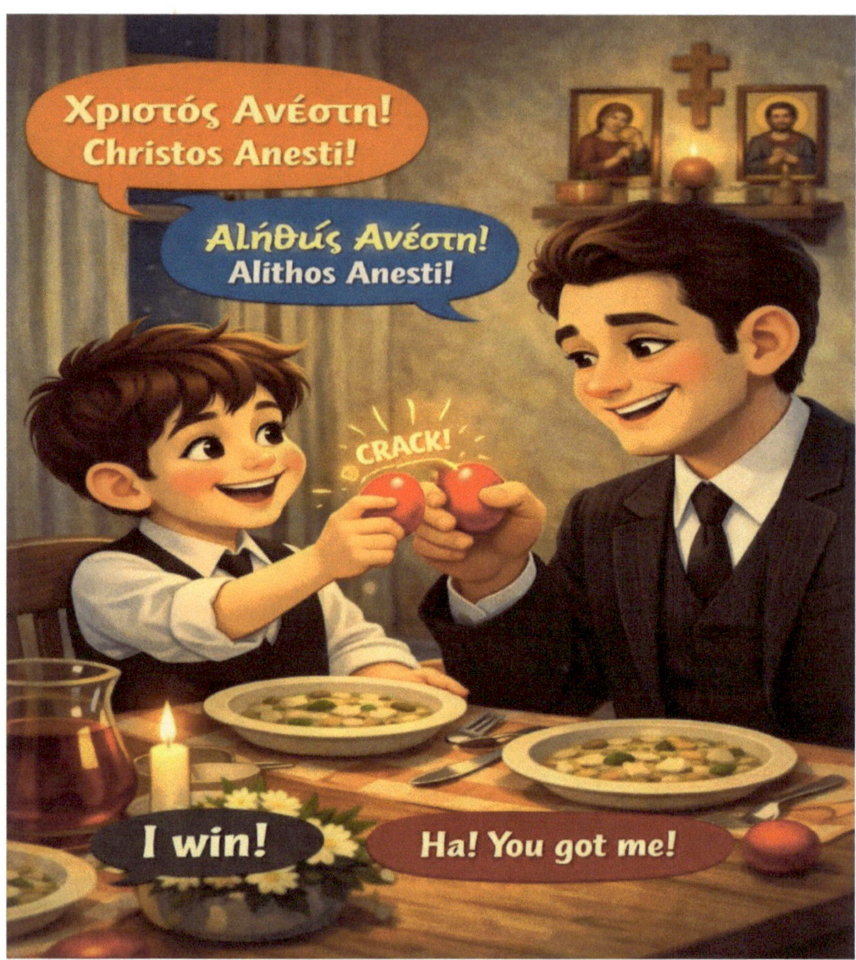


Ari held his red egg tightly, eyes sparkling as he squared off with Uncle Nick across the table. Everyone paused their eating for a moment, watching the two of them with amused anticipation. “Ready, champ?” Nick teased, lifting his egg with a dramatic flourish. Ari grinned, leaning forward. “I’m gonna win this time!” With a sharp crack, the eggs collided and Uncle Nick’s shattered instantly. Ari gasped, then burst into triumphant laughter. “I told you! I told you I’d win!” Nick threw his head back laughing, shaking his head. “Alright, alright, you got me! You’re too strong this year.” Ari puffed up proudly, holding his unbroken egg like a trophy while the whole family chuckled around them, the joy of Easter filling the room as warmly as the candlelight lit.

Laughter bubbled around the table as the egg-cracking battles continued, each CRACK! louder and more dramatic than the last. Ari, still glowing from his victory over Uncle Nick, leaned across the table to challenge Melanie next. “Come on, Aunty Melanie, let’s see what you’ve got!” he said, holding his egg like a tiny warrior. Melanie raised hers with a playful smirk. “Alright, little man, don’t get too confident.” Everyone leaned in as their eggs collided, the sound sharp and satisfying. Ari’s egg stayed strong, and he burst into giggles. “I win again!” he shouted, while Melanie threw her hands up in mock defeat. Nicholas chimed in, “This kid’s unstoppable tonight!” Yia-Yia Dimi just smiled, watching her family tease, laugh, and celebrate, the red eggs tapping like tiny bells of joy. It was the perfect end to a long, holy journey, Easter warmth filling the room, one crack at a time.

Ari leaned in close, gripping his red egg with all the determination a little boy could muster. “Okay, Mummy… this time I’m gonna win,” he declared, narrowing his eyes in playful concentration. Betty smiled, lifting her egg gently. “Let’s see, my love… ready?” The family watched, holding their breath as the two eggs met with a sharp CRACK! Ari’s face fell instantly his egg had shattered while his mum’s stayed perfectly whole. “Aww… no fair…” he muttered, lower lip wobbling just a little. Betty laughed softly and pulled him into a warm hug. “It’s alright, koukla mou… it’s just a game. And you were so brave to challenge me.” Nicholas clapped from across the table. “Come on, Ari, you beat all of us earlier! Your luck had to run out sometime!” Slowly, Ari’s pout melted into a shy smile, the room filling again with laughter, teasing, and the soft glow of Easter joy.

As Ari's eyes grew heavy and the warmth of the long Easter night wrapped around him, the memory of the egg-cracking game with his mum replayed in his mind like a little movie. He could still hear the sharp CRACK! of their eggs meeting, still see his own egg breaking while hers stayed strong, and still feel that tiny sting of disappointment. But as he drifted deeper into sleep, the scene began to soften and shimmer, turning from a real moment into something dreamlike. The table faded, the candlelight stretched into stars, and suddenly the red eggs around him began to glow like tiny lanterns. In his dream, the cracked egg in his hand didn't make him sad anymore, it opened like a magical doorway. Ari stepped through it and found himself on an adventure, carried by the same playful energy he'd shared with his mum at the table. The laughter of his family echoed like music behind him, guiding him forward. What began as a moment of losing became the beginning of a journey, reminding him even in sleep that love, tradition, and a little bit of magic always follow him wherever he goes.

As Ari drifted deeper into sleep, the last flicker of candlelight from the Easter table still warm in his mind, a soft tap-tap-tap echoed against his bedroom window. At first, it blended into his dream, but then it grew clearer gentle, rhythmic. Ari opened his eyes just enough to see a large, friendly face peering in from the night sky. It was an emerald-green dragon with warm golden eyes and a smile that made the whole window glow. Ari sat up slowly, rubbing his eyes, unsure if he was awake or dreaming. Before he could speak, Stinky, Smelly, and Sniffy no longer stuffed and silents sprang to life beside him. The Dragon lowered his head to the window, his voice gentle but trembling with worry. "Ari… my egg has been taken from my cave. I can't find it alone. Will you help me?" And just like that, the disappointment of losing the egg-cracking game with his mum melted away. Ari felt a spark of courage rise in his chest. This wasn't just a dream it was the beginning of an adventure. With his three loyal companions at his side and a dragon waiting at his window, Ari stepped forward into the night, ready to begin the quest to find the stolen Septarian Dragon Egg

The adventure paused for a moment as Ari, the Dragon, and the three lively bears gathered beneath the shimmering night sky. The Dragon lowered his head, his voice softer now, filled with something deeper than worry. "Ari… the Septarian Dragon Egg that was stolen… it wasn't just any egg. It came from Papou Costa and Yia-Yia Dimi's old Poultry farm Nezday ™." Ari's eyes widened. He knew that name. He had heard the stories, the memories, the laughter tied to that land. Stinky stepped forward, ears perked. "Nezday ™ wasn't just a farm it was part of the Makaronis legacy..." Sniffy pointed toward the sky, where the stars began to swirl like a giant clock. "We need to travel back in time to find out when it was taken… and who took it." Ari felt a spark of pride rise in his chest. This wasn't just a quest for a dragon's egg anymore. The Dragon spread his wings, the wind glowing around them. "Your family's legacy must live on, Ari. And to protect it, we must go back to where it all began."

With a deep breath and his friends beside him, Ari stepped forward as the world around them began to shift, ready to journey through time to uncover the truth hidden in Nezday's ™past. High above the glowing clouds, Dean's wings beat steadily as Ari and the three bears huddled together on his back, the wind warm and sparkling with stardust. Below them, the world shimmered like a memory waiting to be rediscovered. "We're getting close to Nezday, ™" Dean rumbled, glancing back with a hopeful smile. Stinky held onto Ari's arm. "Imagine… Papou Costa's farm, but in the past!" Smelly's eyes sparkled. "We might see how the egg was kept safe before it vanished." Sniffy leaned forward, pointing toward the horizon where the outline of a familiar poultry farm floated like an island in the sky. "This is more than a quest," he said softly. "We're protecting the family legacy name." Ari felt his heart swell with pride. "Then let's do it," he said, voice steady. "Let's find out who stole the egg… and why." And together, soaring through the night toward the sky-bound Nezday ™ farm, their adventure truly began.

The Dragon lowered his head gently, the orange glow of sunset casting a soft shimmer across his wings. “I have to go now,” he said, his voice low but steady. “But I’ll return when the time is right.” Ari looked up, eyes wide with questions, but Dean smiled reassuringly. “They know who you are, Ari. They’ve always known. You carry the name, the heart, the legacy.”Stinky stepped closer, his little paw resting on Ari’s shoulder. “We’ll stay with you,” he said. Smelly nodded, her voice warm. “This part of the journey is yours.” Sniffy sniffed the air, then whispered, “The truth is close. We just need to listen.” As Dean rose into the sky, his wings catching the last light of day, Ari watched him disappear into the clouds, feeling something ancient stir inside him. Your Family name was alive here woven into the soil, the silos, the laughter of his young mum, the steady gaze of Papou Costa. And now, it was Ari’s turn to protect it.

Ari stepped forward slowly, his heart thumping like a tiny drum inside his chest. The golden light of Nezday™ wrapped around everything the barns, the chickens, the silos and then his eyes landed on the man he had only known through stories, photos, and the love in his family's voices. Papou Costa. Strong hands, gentle eyes, standing just as the stories said he would. Before Ari could stop himself, his feet moved on their own. He ran past the sheep, past the chickens, past the warm breeze of the dream-farmand straight into Papou's arms. Papou knelt down just in time, catching him in a hug that felt like home, even though they had never met. Behind them, little-girl Betty gasped, teenage Nick and Melanie stared in wonder, and the three bears whispered, "He found him… he really found him." In that moment, time didn't matter. Legacy did. Love did. And Ari felt it all wrap around him like a warm blanket

Ari stepped forward slowly, his heart thumping like a tiny drum inside his chest. The golden light of Nezday™ wrapped around everything the barns, the chickens, the silos and then his eyes landed on the man he had only known through stories, photos, and the love in his family's voices. Papou Costa. Strong hands, gentle eyes, standing just as the stories said he would. Before Ari could stop himself, his feet moved on their own. He ran past the sheep, past the chickens, past the warm breeze of the dream-farm and straight into Papou's arms. Papou knelt down just in time, catching him in a hug that felt like home, even though they had never met. Behind them, little-girl Betty gasped, teenage Nick and Melanie stared in wonder, and the three bears whispered, "He found him… he really found him." In that moment, time didn't matter. Legacy did. Love did. And Ari felt it all wrap around him like a warm blanket.

There stood Next to Papou Costa his  two favourite Dogs  Spiro The Kelpie and Max the short Haired  Pointer, his eyes softening the moment Ari ran into his arms. He held him close, one strong hand on the back of Ari's head, as if he had been waiting for this hug his whole life. When he finally leaned back to look at Ari's face, there was a warmth there that felt ancient and familiar all at once."Ari mou… I know you. I've known you long before you were born," Papou said, his voice deep and gentle, carrying the calm of the farm and the strength of the Family  name. "You carry our heart… our story… our legacy. And now you've come all this way to find the truth. I'm proud of you, paidi mou. So proud."Ari felt something glow inside him like he had stepped into a place he belonged, even though he had never been here before. Papou brushed a thumb across his cheek and smiled. "Come… there is much I want to show you. And even more you are meant to discover."

Papou Costa gently took Ari's hand and led him toward the old chicken coop, the golden light casting long shadows across the Nezday™ farm. "This," he said, pointing to a small hollow nestled beneath the coop's wooden beams, "is where the Septarian Dragon Egg once rested." Ari knelt beside it, eyes wide, tracing the outline of the space with his fingers. It shimmered faintly, as if the egg's memory still pulsed in the soil. "It was protected here for generations," Papou continued, his voice low and reverent. "Until someone came… someone who knew its power and took it." Ari looked up, heart pounding. "We'll find it, Papou. I promise." Papou smiled, placing a hand on Ari's shoulder. "You already carry its light, Ari mou. Now let's uncover the truth."

Papou Costa crouched beside the old wooden beam, brushing away a layer of hay with his weathered hands. "This," he said, voice thick with memory, "is where the Septarian Egg once rested. It wasn't just any egg it was a family heirloom. My father gave it to me, and now…" He looked at Ari with eyes full of pride, "It's yours." Ari's breath caught. The space beneath the coop shimmered faintly, as if the egg's magic still lingered.

Behind them, Aunty Melanie swept the barn floor, pausing mid-stroke as she overheard Papou's words. Her eyes softened, and she gave Ari a quiet nod of encouragement. Outside, the two horses Blacky, the proud black stallion, and Snow, the gentle white mare were being fed, their saddles ready. "They'll take you," Papou said, rising slowly. "They know the land, the legends, and the way forward. But only you can find what was lost."

Papou's voice carried a warmth that filled the whole barn as he guided Ari's small hands toward the horses. "These two," he said, offering a carrot to Blacky, "have been with our family longer than you can imagine." Snow, the gentle white mare, nudged Ari's shoulder as if greeting an old friend. Aunty Melanie paused her sweeping, leaning on the broom with a soft smile as she watched the moment unfold. Papou continued, "The Septarian Egg… it wasn't just a treasure. It was passed to me by my father, and now, Ari mou, it belongs to you." Ari looked up, eyes wide, feeling the weight of the legacy settle into his chest. Blacky snorted proudly, Snow stamped her hoof, and Papou chuckled. "They're ready to take you wherever you need to go. They know the land, the stories, and the secrets. And now, they'll help you find what was lost. Ari turned to the horses, heart pounding with purpose. The journey was calling.

Ari stood beside the long rows of nesting boxes, the warm scent of straw and feathers wrapping around him like a memory he hadn't lived yet. Beside him, a young Yia-Yia Dimi, her hair tied back in a neat ribbon, her hands quick and gentle showed him how to lift each egg with care. "Always treat them like treasure, Ari," she said softly, her voice full of the same kindness he knew from the future. The hens clucked around them, the shed glowing with golden light as dust motes drifted like tiny stars. Ari watched her closely, realizing he wasn't just collecting egg she was collecting pieces of his family's story. And in that quiet moment, standing shoulder-to-shoulder with the girl who would one day become his Yia-Yia, he felt the past and present fold together like two hands meeting in a promise.

Ari stood beside Uncle Nick in the cool room, the air humming softly with the machines and the faint chill brushing their cheeks. Trays of eggs stretched out in perfect rows, and Uncle Nick—fresh out of high school, still carrying that mix of excitement and uncertainty—handled each egg like it was something precious. Ari watched him with wide eyes. "You're really good at this," he said. Nick let out a small laugh, shaking his head. "Good? I'm just learning, little man. This is all new to me." He lifted an egg to the light, studying it the way Papou had taught him only days before. "I finished school last week… and now I'm here, trying to figure out what comes next." Ari tilted his head. "Do you like it?" Nick paused, the question landing deeper than Ari expected. "I think… I'm trying to," he admitted. "It's different. Grown-up different. I am a city Boy, not a country boy!" He glanced down at Ari, a softer smile forming. "But having you here makes it feel less scary." Ari grinned, holding up an egg proudly. "We can learn together." Nick ruffled his hair, warmth finally reaching his eyes. "Yeah. I'd like that."

Papou's voice carried across the yard, strong and certain, cutting through the warm glow of the sunset. "It's time to go, Ari!" he called, his hand raised as the chariot gleamed behind him. Blacky and Snow stood harnessed and ready, their great wings folded neatly at their sides, feathers shimmering like they held the last light of the day. The chariot itself seemed alive its wooden frame humming with old magic, its red cushions waiting for the boy destined to sit upon them. Ari felt his heart leap, not with fear, but with purpose. Papou stepped closer, resting a steady hand on his shoulder. "The Septarian Egg Crystal is out there, waiting for the one brave enough to find it. The chariot awaits you, grandson… for a safe and prosperous journey." Ari climbed aboard, the bears scrambling in beside him, and as the horses pawed at the cobblestones, he knew this was the moment everything changed.

The chariot rose slowly at first, the wings of Blacky and Snow beating against the glowing air as the golden portal widened before them. Ari held tight to the rail, his heart racing with a mix of fear and wonder. Below, the whole farm gathered Papou, Yia-Yia Dimi, Uncle Nick, Aunty Melanie, the animals, even the chickens waving with all their love behind their hands. "Safe travels, Ari! Good luck!" their voices echoed up toward him, carried by the warm evening breeze. Then, from the far side of the yard, came the sound of hurried footsteps. Betty burst out of the barn, breathless, her hair flying behind her. She hadn't had a moment with Ari not today, not with all the work she'd been left to shoulder while everyone else moved on. She ran as fast as she could, her voice cracking as she shouted, "See you on the other side, Ari! Be careful!" Ari twisted in the chariot, eyes wide, lifting his hand high to wave back. For a heartbeat, their eyes met hers full of longing and unspoken stories, his full of promise. And then the chariot surged upward, light swirling around them, carrying him toward the unknown while Betty stood below, her hand pressed to her heart, whispering her goodbye into the wind.

Ari stepped carefully onto the ancient stones, his flashlight beam dancing across the carved steps as the bears clustered around him. Stinky tugged at his sleeve. "So… this is Greece?" he whispered, eyes wide. Ari nodded, unfolding the map. "Yeah. Papou said the first clue would be somewhere old… somewhere important." Smelly lifted her little light toward the towering columns. "These look pretty important," she said proudly. Sniffy sniffed the air dramatically. "I smell history. And maybe… olives." Ari laughed, shaking his head.Just then, the chariot wheels scraped softly against the stone as Blacky and Snow settled behind them. "We made it, Ari," Snow said gently, her wings folding with a soft rustle. "Where to next?" Blacky asked, stamping his hoof with excitement. Ari looked up at the glowing ruins, the sunset painting everything gold. "We start here," he said, voice steady with purpose. "Somewhere in these stones… the past is waiting to talk to us."Above them, the little dragon swooped low, scattering sparks like blessings. The adventure had truly begun.

A sudden crack of lightning split the sky as Athena descended in a shimmer of gold, her wings unfolding like living light above the ancient stones. Ari felt the air shift warm, powerful, ancient as of his Ancestors past had come to life. The goddess of wisdom regarded him with eyes that held every story ever told. "Ari," she said, her voice both gentle and thunderous, "you walk a path older than your name, older even than the Egg you seek." A glowing key drifted from her hand, lowering toward him like a blessing. Stinky, Smelly, and Sniffy watched in trembling awe while the little dragon circled overhead. Shimmering lights spiralled around them like falling stars, painting the ruins in gold and silver. Ari froze, breath caught in his chest, mesmerised by the whole damn lie he'd been told about the world being ordinary. As he reached for the key, he knew nothing about his life would ever be the same again.

Ari stood before the cave carved into the ancient rock, the Acropolis glowing behind him like a guardian watching from above. "This must be where the surprise is hiding," he whispered, gripping the golden key Athena had given him. The bears huddled close as he stepped toward the towering stone gate. When Ari lifted the key, it pulsed with warm light then the entire doorway answered. Ancient symbols along the stone began to glow like stars waking from a long sleep. A deep rumble shook the mountain as the key slid into a hidden lock, turning on its own. With a burst of golden sparks, the massive gates opened, revealing a chamber swirling with light and secrets. There, at the heart of the chamber, stood the Caduceus radiant, suspended above its pedestal as if breathing with ancient life. Ari felt a pull deep in his chest. This wasn't just an object; it was a symbol of healing, truth, balance, and the power to rise after every fall. The twin serpents shimmered like living wisdom, reflecting the light of every ancestor who had walked this land. In that moment, Ari understood: the Caduceus hadn't simply been waiting to be found. It had been waiting for him the one destined to restore what had been lost since the collapse of the Nezday dynasty.

Ari lifted the Caduceus high, its golden light spilling across the cliffs as Hermes stepped from the glowing doorway in a rush of wind and stardust. “So,” the god said with a knowing smile, “the boy who carries the key… and now the staff.” The Caduceus pulsed in Ari’s hands like a heartbeat. “You’ve awakened a path only the brave dare can walk.” Then Hermes’ voice softened. “Your mother, Betty, stood here long before you brave, determined, carrying questions heavier than her years. Send her my love for returning to clear the secret she once uncovered with the Prince of Peace. She walked this path so you could finish what she began.” Ari felt her courage settle beside his own, not as a burden, but as a torch passed from one generation to the next.

Hermes stepped into the swirling doorway, stardust rising like wind. "Your next step awaits far from here," he said. "Follow the Caduceus, Ari. It knows the way." The staff pulsed brighter, its serpents lifting their heads. A warm gust swept through the cave, tugging at Ari's clothes. Blacky and Snow landed at the cliff's edge, wings unfurled. The bears scrambled aboard, the dragon roared overhead, and Ari climbed into the chariot, the Caduceus blazing in his grip. With one mighty beat of wings, they soared into the sky Greece fading behind them, Egypt glowing ahead, golden and full of secrets.

As the golden sun dipped behind the pyramids, casting long shadows across the desert, Ari stepped forward, heart thudding, the Caduceus glowing in his hand. Before him stood Thoth, radiant and timeless, his ibis gaze filled with ancient knowing. With a graceful motion, the god extended a glowing ankh toward Ari a symbol of life, truth, and divine memory. "This is not just Egypt," Thoth said, his voice like wind over stone. "This is where stories are remembered, and destinies are rewritten." Stinky, Smelly, and Sniffy watched in reverent silence, the desert around them shimmering with possibility. Ari reached out, knowing this gift would unlock more than secrets it would awaken the legacy his mother once touched, and guide him deeper into the mythic truth of who he was becoming.

As the sun dipped low behind the pyramids, the desert glowed with ancient fire. Ari and the bears approached the towering stone wall when, without warning, the ankh in Smelly's paws ignited with golden light. The pyramid trembled softly, as though recognizing an old friend. With a gentle click, the ankh unlocked a hidden doorway, and a radiant beam spilled out across the sand. Ari felt the warmth of destiny brush his face this was no ordinary entrance, but a passage only the worthy could open. Stinky, Smelly, and Sniffy stood proudly at his side as the golden door widened, inviting them into the secrets Egypt had guarded for thousands of years.

The moment Ari and the bears stepped inside the pyramid, the air grew still, as if the ancient walls were listening. Golden light danced across the hieroglyphs, revealing stories carved long before their time. Stinky, Smelly, and Sniffy traced the symbols with wide-eyed wonder. "Look," Ari whispered, brushing his fingers over the carvings, "it's telling a story." Stinky pointed at a bird-headed figure. "That looks like the one who gave you the key!" Smelly tapped a glowing sun symbol. "This one feels like life." Sniffy found a carving of a serpent-twined staff. "Ari… that's your Caduceus." Ari felt a shiver of awe. "Maybe these aren't just pictures," he murmured. "Maybe they're instructions… meant for us." And the chamber seemed to hum in quiet agreement.

Ari and the bears stepped deeper into the chamber, their breath catching as the golden sarcophagus came into view majestic, ancient, and glowing softly as though it recognized their arrival. Stinky, Smelly, and Sniffy huddled close, their eyes darting between the carved pharaoh and the shimmering artifact resting in the glass case beside him. “Look at that eye,” Sniffy whispered, pointing to the radiant symbol. “It’s watching us.” Ari felt the same strange pull he’d felt with the Caduceus and the ankh a sense that these weren’t just relics, but pieces of a puzzle meant for them. The hieroglyphs surrounding the sarcophagus seemed to shift in the warm light, telling a story older than memory itself. Ari swallowed, heart pounding. Whatever secret Egypt had guarded for thousands of years… they were standing right in front of it.

Stinky held up the ruby Eye of Horus, its red glow flickering like a tiny flame. "Ari… this one feels warm," he said, eyes wide. "Like it's alive." Smelly stepped beside him, cradling the emerald-green Eye. "And mine feels different," she whispered. "Cool… like calm water." Ari looked between them, feeling the relics hum in the air. "The red eye," he murmured, "must be the Eye of Protection strength, courage, fire." The ruby shimmered brighter, as if agreeing. "And the green one," Ari continued, touching Smelly's gem, "that's healing… truth… the heart of Horus." A soft breeze stirred through the chamber though no door was open, carrying a whisper of ancient magic. Sniffy gasped. "Ari… I think the pyramid knows we've found the right ones." And for a moment, the whole tomb seemed to glow welcoming them deeper into its secret.

With the relics safely tucked away, the desert wind rose again this time carrying the promise of their next adventure. The golden chariot waited outside the pyramid, already glowing with fresh magic. A winged guardian stood at the reins, feathers shimmering like sunlight on water, ready to guide them onward. Ari scrambled up onto the white horse, gripping its mane as it pawed eagerly at the sand. Above them, the dragon swooped low with an excited roar, circling like a signal flare in the sky. Stinky, Sleepy, and Sniffy hurried after Ari, their little paws kicking up dust as they raced toward the chariot. "Come on!" Ari called, laughter in his voice. "The journey's not over yet!" And with a burst of wind and wings, they lifted off toward whatever mystery awaited them next.

The golden chariot soared over Rome as the sunset painted the city in molten gold, and Ari leaned over the edge, eyes wide. "Look down there!" he shouted. "That's the Colosseum—it's huge!" Stinky pressed his paws to the rail. "And that round building with the giant hole in the roof… that must be the Pantheon!" Sleepy pointed toward a long stretch of ancient stone. "Ari, that's the Roman Forum—it looks like a whole city made of ruins." Sniffy sniffed the air, tail twitching. "And over there… the Trevi Fountain! I can smell the water from up here." The winged horses dipped lower as the dragon circled joyfully above them, and the guardian called out, "Hold on, travellers Rome is ready for you." Ari grinned at the bears. "Get ready. We're about to land in history itself."

The chariot dipped out of the clouds and landed beside the shimmering Trevi Fountain, golden dust swirling around their feet as Ari and the bears hopped down. "Whoa… this isn't Egypt anymore," Ari whispered, staring at the towering statues of Oceanus and the rushing water that had granted wishes for centuries. Stinky spun in a circle. "Ari, this place looks like someone sprinkled magic everywhere!" Sleepy pointed at the glowing water. "It's sparkling… just like the pyramid did." Sniffy sniffed the air. "New smells, new magic. We've definitely landed in a city." The winged guardian folded his radiant wings with a gentle smile. "Welcome to Rome where travellers have tossed coins for luck for over two hundred years." Above them, the dragon swooped low in a cheerful arc, as if saying you made it. Ari squeezed Shiffy's paw. "Come on, everyone. If Egypt had secrets… imagine what this place is hiding." And together they stepped into Rome's golden light, ready for the adventure waiting just ahead.

Ari stood at the edge of the ancient stones, the warm Roman sun dipping low behind the broken columns of the Roman Forum, and the bears gathered close, their eyes wide with awe. "So, this is where emperors actually walked?" Stinky whispered, staring at the towering ruins glowing gold in the sunset. Smelly brushed her paw along a weathered pillar. "It feels… old, but alive. Like it remembers everything." Sniffy sniffed the air, tail twitching. "History smells dusty… but also kind of magical." Ari smiled, taking in the arches, the domes, the echoes of a world long gone. "This place shaped the whole world," he said softly. "And now we're standing right in the middle of it." Together, they stepped forward into the ancient heart of Rome, ready for whatever secret the stones might share next.

Ari and the bears followed the cobblestone path until the ancient walls rose before them, glowing gold in the late Roman sun. "Whoa…" Ari whispered, staring up at the towering arches of the Colosseum. Stinky's mouth fell, open. "Ari, it's huge! Did real gladiators fight in there?" Smelly clutched her pink dress, eyes wide. "It feels… powerful. Like the stones are still telling stories." Sniffy sniffed the warm air thoughtfully. "Smells like dust, history… and maybe gelato or Salami Mozzarella Pizza with olives somewhere nearby." Ari laughed softly, stepping closer to the ancient arena. "This place is almost two thousand years old," he said. "Imagine all the people who stood right where we're standing now." Together, they gazed up at the mighty Colosseum, feeling the weight of history and the thrill of adventure settle gently around them as Rome opened its arms to their next discovery.

Ari stepped into the golden beam of light, the ancient hall glowing as if it had been waiting centuries just for this moment. The majestic woman in shimmering Armor the Goddess Athena. Her presence here didn't break the story it deepened it. It showed that Ari's journey wasn't tied to one country or one mythology, but to something older and wiser, something that connected Greece, Egypt, Rome, and every ancient place touched by magic. Athena lowered herself gracefully to one knee before him, her eyes warm and full of knowing. "Ari," she said softly, "you have carried this key with courage." The glowing key pulsed in his hands, as if recognizing her. Stinky, Smelly, and Sniffy stood frozen in awe, their little paws clasped together. Above them, the great owl circled through the light, feathers sparkling like stars. Ari took a steady breath and held out the key, and as she accepted it, the whole chamber brightened columns humming, dust turning to gold, the air alive with ancient magic. In that instant, Ari felt it: he wasn't just giving her a key… he was unlocking the next part of his destiny.

The moment Athena's key touched the air, a brilliant whirl of golden light burst open above Ari, spinning into a shimmering portal that hummed with ancient power. Symbols of Rome flickered around him before dissolving into stars, and the green dragon swooped down through the glow with a joyful roar, its wings scattering sparks across the hall. "Ari!" Stinky cried, pointing upward. "The path is opening!" The bears huddled close as the wind from the portal rushed past them, warm and full of promise. Ari felt the pull of destiny tug at his chest gentle, certain, calling him forward. The dragon dipped low, inviting him onto its back. Ari turned to the bears with a grin. "Time to go," he said. "Our next adventure is waiting… Jerusalem." And with one leap into the swirling light, they soared toward the next chapter of their journey.

Ari slid off the dragon's back as they touched down on the rocky hilltop, the warm Jerusalem breeze brushing past them like a welcome. Below, the golden city shimmered in the sunset, rooftops glowing and doves circling gently through the sky. Stinky, Smelly, and Sniffy stepped forward, paws clasped, their eyes wide with wonder. The dragon folded its wings and settled beside them, gazing proudly at the glowing dome in the distance. Ari felt his heart lift this place felt ancient, peaceful, and full of stories waiting to be discovered. "We made it," he whispered, the light dancing across his face. "Jerusalem… the next part of our adventure begins here."

Ari drifted down on a soft cloud with Stinky, Smelly, and Sniffy tucked close beside him, the night sky glowing with a single bright star that seemed to call his name. Below them, a warm golden light shimmered over a tiny stable, where a newborn baby lay surrounded by love and quiet wonder. Shepherds watched in awe, animals rested peacefully, and the whole world felt still, as if holding its breath for this moment. Ari felt his heart glow. "This is where hope began," he whispered, and the bears nodded, their eyes shining as the star above them sparkled even brighter.

Ari sat quietly on the sunlit rock, above that mountain. The breeze carrying the scent of flowers as he watched the glowing figure ahead welcome the children with open arms. Hearts of light floated gently through the sky, and doves circled above as if they understood the kindness being shared below. Stinky, Smelly, and Sniffy nestled close beside him, their eyes wide with wonder. Ari felt something soft and steady settle in his chest  a feeling of peace, like the world itself was reminding him to lead with love. "This is what he taught," Ari whispered. "Kindness… for everyone." And the meadow seemed to glow even brighter.

Ari stepped carefully through the field of glowing flowers, their petals shimmering like tiny stars beneath his feet. The radiant figure knelt among the blossoms, hands outstretched, a soft smile lighting the air around him. In his palms rested a small, shining key that pulsed with warmth, as if it already knew Ari's heart. Stinky, Smelly, and Sniffy huddled close behind him, their eyes wide with awe. Ari felt a peaceful hush settle over the world as he reached out. When the key touched his hand, the whole meadow brightened, and Ari understood this was a gift of guidance, a reminder that love and light would lead him on the next step of his journey.

Ari led the way through the field of glowing flowers, the morning light brushing the world in soft gold as the great stone tomb came into view. Stinky, Smelly, and Sniffy stayed close behind him, their paws clasped in quiet excitement. The stone at the entrance shimmered faintly, as if waiting for him. Ari reached into his pocket and pulled out the radiant key the gift he had been entrusted with. As he stepped forward, the key warmed in his hand, glowing brighter with every heartbeat. He touched it gently to the edge of the stone, and a soft burst of light rippled outward. With a deep, peaceful hum, the tomb opened, filling the air with warmth and hope. Ari felt it instantly this was not an ending, but the beginning of something new.

Ari shielded his eyes as the tomb opened, a soft golden light pouring out and rising into the sky. Stinky, Smelly, and Sniffy gasped as a glowing cross appeared above the city, shining like a promise. "What does it mean, Ari?" Sniffy whispered. Ari stepped forward, feeling the warmth of the light settle in his chest. "It means love," he said softly. "The kind that never gives up." Stinky nodded slowly. "So… it's not about being scared?" Ari shook his head. "No. It's about someone loving the world so much that light became stronger than darkness." Smelly squeezed her paws together. "For everyone?" Ari smiled. "For everyone." And as the cross glowed brighter, they all stood together, understanding that this moment wasn't about sorrow it was about hope, forgiveness, and a love big enough to guide every step of their journey.

As they walked closer to the glowing cross, the light grew brighter not harsh, but inviting, like a warm hug from the sky. Ari felt a gentle surge through his spine, like electricity made of love, guiding him toward something sacred. The energy drifted around them, soft and golden, and it was as if the light itself reached out and handed Ari the divine. Just then, Sniffy paused beside a rock, his eyes catching the sparkle of something extraordinary nestled among the flowers. "Look!" he called softly, waving Ari and the others over. Smelly leaned in, her voice hushed with wonder. "It's a cross… but not just any cross." Emeralds and rubies glowed from its golden frame, like tiny stars stitched into a treasure. Stinky blinked. "It looks like it's been waiting for us." Sniffy reached out and touched it gently, feeling warmth pulse through his paws. "I think it's meant for Ari," he said, turning toward the boy. Ari stepped closer, heart thudding with quiet awe. "Then let's carry it with care," he whispered. "It's part of the story now." And the light from the sky seemed to nod in agreement reminding them all that the true meaning of the Cross was love, freely given, and meant to be shared.

Smelly leaned gently over the rock, her little paws brushing against the beautiful cross nestled in the sunlight. Emeralds and rubies sparkled like stars, and the gold shimmered with a quiet glow. “It’s waiting for you,” she whispered, lifting it carefully. Sniffy stepped forward, holding out his paws. “Let me give it to him,” he said softly. Ari knelt down, eyes wide, as Sniffy placed the cross into his hands. “This isn’t just treasure,” Ari said, feeling its weight. “It’s a reminder that love is the strongest light.” He opened his backpack and tucked the cross inside, close to his heart. Stinky nodded. “We’ll carry it with us. Together.” And as the glowing cross in the sky watched over them, the four friends stood united, ready for whatever came next.

All at once, the ground beneath them hummed, and a swirling golden wind wrapped around Ari, Stinky, Smelly, and Sniffy like a living ribbon of light. Flowers lifted from the earth, spinning upward as the breeze grew into a shimmering tornado not wild or frightening, but warm and full of wonder. "Hold on!" Stinky shouted, grabbing Ari's sleeve as Smelly clutched Sniffy's paw. The world around them blurred into sparkles, Jerusalem fading into a soft glow while a new landscape formed in the spinning light. Lanterns, cherry blossoms, and ancient rooftops appeared as if painted by the wind itself. Ari felt his heart leap they weren't falling; they were being carried. "We're entering the next realm," he whispered. And with a final swirl of golden magic, the tornado gently set them down in the mystical lands of China, where dragons watched from the mountains and a new chapter of their dream awaited.

They landed softly in a valley of cherry blossoms, their petals drifting like pink snow as lanterns swayed gently in the warm breeze. Ancient rooftops curved toward the sky, and the air shimmered with a quiet, sacred energy. From the mist rose the true dragon not the playful guide they had met before, but his real, majestic form: long, emerald-scaled, crowned with antlers, and glowing with wisdom older than mountains. Yet his presence wasn't frightening. It felt peaceful, like meeting a guardian of the earth itself. Ari, Stinky, Smelly, and Sniffy stood in awe as the dragon bowed his great head. "In China," Ari whispered, "the dragon isn't a monster… he's a symbol of strength, protection, and harmony." The dragon's golden eyes softened, as if agreeing. He represented balance the breath of life, the bridge between heaven and earth and now he had come to guide them on the next sacred step of their journey.

Ari, Stinky, Smelly, and Sniffy found themselves standing on the ancient stones of the Great Wall of China, high above mist-covered mountains that rolled like waves beneath the rising sun. Cherry blossoms drifted through the air, carried by a gentle breeze that smelled of spring and old magic. “Where are we now?” Smelly whispered, clutching Sniffy’s paw. Before Ari could answer, a deep, peaceful rumble echoed through the valley. From the mist emerged the great dragon long, emerald-scaled, and glowing softly as he curled through the mountains like living wind. Stinky stepped closer, eyes wide. “He’s not here to scare us,” Ari said calmly. The dragon lowered his head, golden eyes warm and wise. “I guide those who walk with courage,” his voice seemed to say without words. “Here in China, I am the spirit of strength, balance, and protection.” And with a slow, graceful sweep of his tail, he beckoned them forward along the Wall, inviting them to follow him into the next chapter of their journey.

Ari, Stinky, Smelly, and Sniffy sat safely on the dragon's back as he glided above the misty Li River, the golden sunset painting the karst mountains in soft light. Tiny boats drifted below like floating lanterns, and cherry blossoms swirled through the air as if welcoming them. "This place… it feels like a dream," Smelly whispered, holding Sniffy's paw. The dragon's deep voice rumbled kindly beneath them. "You are in Guilin, the land where mountains touch the sky and the river remembers ancient stories." Stinky leaned forward, eyes wide. "Are you taking us somewhere special?" The dragon nodded, his emerald scales shimmering. "I guide those who seek truth and courage. Here, in China, I am the spirit of wisdom, balance, and the breath of life." Ari smiled, feeling the wind lift his hair. "Then lead the way," he said softly. And with a graceful sweep of his wings, the dragon carried them deeper into the glowing valley, toward the next lesson their journey was ready to reveal.

Ari, Stinky, Smelly, and Sniffy stood on the stone path overlooking a peaceful valley in China, where cherry blossoms drifted like soft pink snow and lanterns glowed beneath the golden sunset. Pagodas rose gently from the hills, and a quiet river wound through the village like a silver ribbon. "It feels… calm here," Smelly whispered, squeezing Sniffy's paw. Stinky nodded. "Like the world is telling us to slow down and listen." Ari breathed in the warm air, sensing something sacred in the stillness. "This place," he said softly, "is where wisdom lives." The dragon's presence lingered in the air, guiding them even when unseen a reminder that strength doesn't always roar; sometimes it arrives as peace, balance, and the courage to keep walking. Together, they stepped forward, knowing this moment was another gentle lesson in their unfolding journey.

There, in the heart of the moonlit garden, stood the Pearl of Harmony glowing softly atop its ancient pedestal, as if holding the breath of the world inside it. Cherry blossoms drifted around it like falling stars, and beside the shimmering orb stood a small white bunny rabbit, calm and wise, its fur glowing in the moonlight. Ari, Stinky, Smelly, and Sniffy stepped closer, feeling the air grow still and peaceful. “Is… is that the Moon Rabbit?” Smelly whispered. The bunny nodded gently, eyes warm and knowing. “This pearl,” Ari murmured, “it’s not just light… it’s balance, kindness, and the power to heal.” The rabbit placed a tiny paw on the pedestal, and the Pearl brightened, filling the garden with a soft, loving glow. In that moment, they understood  this realm was teaching them harmony, the strength that comes not from force, but from gentleness, and unity.

Ari, Stinky, Smelly, and Sniffy stepped through the blossom-covered archway and found themselves in a moonlit garden unlike anything they had seen before. At the centre stood the Pearl of Harmony, glowing softly in the night air as if holding the heartbeat of the whole realm inside it. Beside the pearl sat a small white rabbit, calm and luminous, its ears twitching as it watched them with ancient understanding. “Is he guarding it?” Stinky whispered. The rabbit gave a slow nod, as though saying that harmony must always be protected. Ari felt the stillness settle into his chest a peaceful reminder that balance, kindness, and unity were just as powerful as courage. Smelly leaned closer to the pearl, her voice barely a breath. “It feels like it’s healing the whole world.” And as the moonlight shimmered across the garden, the rabbit stepped aside, inviting them to learn the quiet strength that comes from a heart at peace.

Ari knelt beneath the moonlit archway, the air warm with drifting cherry blossoms and the soft glow of lanterns reflecting on the still water beyond. The great garden felt sacred, as though time itself had paused to watch. In front of him, the Moon Rabbit held out the Pearl of Harmony with gentle paws, its light pulsing like a quiet heartbeat. Smelly, Stinky, and Sniffy stood close behind, hardly daring to breathe. "He's giving it to you," Sniffy whispered, eyes wide with wonder. Ari reached out, feeling a peaceful warmth flow through his fingers the moment he touched the glowing orb. The rabbit's gaze was kind, ancient, as if saying, this is for the one who walks with courage and kindness. Ari held the pearl to his chest, understanding that this gift wasn't just magic it was trust, balance, and the reminder that harmony begins within.

Ari, Stinky, Smelly, and Sniffy stood on the glowing deck of the little river boat as it drifted through the warm sunset, the water shimmering with lotus lights that seemed to breathe with magic. A rainbow trail stretched across the river ahead of them, as if the sky itself had opened a path just for their journey. "It feels like the world is guiding us somewhere," Smelly whispered, her eyes wide with wonder. Stinky leaned on the railing, watching the colours ripple across the water. "It's peaceful… like the river knows our story." Sniffy nodded, sensing the gentle pull of the current. Ari placed a hand on his backpack, feeling the warmth of the Pearl of Harmony inside. "Every realm teaches us something," he said softly. "Maybe this one is about trust trusting the path, trusting the light, trusting each other." And as the boat glided forward, the rainbow shimmered brighter, welcoming them into the next chapter of their dream.

A warm rush of golden light lifted Ari, Love, Dreamy, and Harmony from the riverbank, swirling around them like a joyful celebration from the heavens. Symbols from every realm they had visited shimmered above their heads the lotus, the flame, the pearl, the crosses, the key  all glowing as if blessing their journey. "What's happening?" Dreamy laughed, spinning gently in the air. Harmony pointed toward the horizon where a magnificent archway shimmered in the sunset. "We're being called forward," he said softly. Ari felt no fear, only excitement, as the rainbow path beneath them brightened and the lotus flowers on the water opened in greeting. "This is the next realm," Ari whispered, clutching his backpack. A land of colour, spirit, and new beginnings." And as the light carried them toward the glowing arch, they knew they were stepping into a place where ancient magic and heart-wisdom waited to meet them.

Ari, Stinky, Smelly, and Sniffy wandered through the glowing Moroccan garden, the deep-blue walls shining like sapphire under the warm sun. Palm trees swayed gently, and lotus flowers floated on the still pond beside them. “This place feels like a dream,” Smelly whispered, brushing her paw along a bright yellow pot. Sniffy sniffed the air. “It smells like flowers and magic.” Stinky looked around, eyes wide. “What are we meant to find here?” Ari paused, feeling the calm settle into his chest. “Maybe this realm is about beauty… and remembering that creativity is also a kind of magic.” And as they walked deeper into the garden, sparkles drifted around them, guiding them toward the next lesson.

Ari, Stinky, Smelly, and Sniffy followed the winding path until it opened into a quiet courtyard where the sunlight pooled like liquid gold. In the centre stood a single ceramic pot plain, unpainted, untouched by colour. It looked almost out of place among the bright blues and blooming flowers. “Why is this one empty?” Stinky asked, tilting his head. Smelly stepped closer, running her paw along its smooth surface. “Maybe… it’s waiting for something.” Sniffy noticed a soft shimmer rising from inside the pot, like a breath of warm light. Ari knelt beside it, feeling a calm warmth spread through his chest. “This is what Morocco wants to show us,” he said softly. “Beauty isn’t just what we see. It’s what we create. What we bring. What we share.” As they touched the pot together, colours bloomed from within pinks, blues, golds swirling upward like paint coming alive. The empty pot filled itself with light, reflecting each of their hearts. And in that moment, they understood: Morocco’s gift was creativity, the reminder that they carry magic inside them, ready to shape the world ahead.

Ari stepped into the glowing courtyard, the blue walls shimmering like twilight water. Stinky, Smelly, and Sniffy pressed close beside him as a warm golden light gathered ahead. From within it, the Guardian of Morocco emerged graceful, radiant, her veil drifting like sunlight made silk. She knelt to meet Ari's eyes, her smile soft and knowing. In that instant, the garden fell silent, as if every flower and stone was holding its breath. Ari felt something settle inside him a calm, a trust, a sense that this was a place where beauty and peace lived together. The Guardian opened her hands, inviting him forward, and the air around them sparkled with quiet magic.

Ari looked up at the Guardian, his hands still open after placing the Cross of Light into hers. She studied the jewelled cross for a moment, then shook her head gently. "You can keep the cross, little one," she said, her voice warm as sunlight. "It is your family's heirloom a gift of courage and love passed through generations. It belongs with you."

Just then, the Pearl of Harmony slipped from Ari's bag and rolled across the stone. The Guardian reached down gracefully, lifting the glowing pearl into her palm. "And this," she whispered, "brings balance and peace wherever it travels." She placed the pearl back into Ari's hands and rested her golden fingers over both treasures. "I bless them both," she said softly. "May light and harmony protect you on every path ahead."

The Guardian placed her golden hands gently over Ari's, her touch warm as sunlight. "Ari," she said softly, "you carry more than treasures. You carry the love of your family, the courage of your ancestors, and the harmony that lives inside your heart." Her veil shimmered as the portal behind her began to glow brighter. "The Cross of Light will remind you who you are. The Pearl of Harmony will remind you how to walk your path. Keep them close, little one." She leaned forward, her voice lowering to a tender whisper. "Wherever you go, may light guide your steps, and may peace follow behind you." She smiled, full of pride and knowing. "India awaits you now. Go with blessing." As the golden portal shimmered open, the Guardian of Morocco stepped forward, her light warm and steady. "Ari," she said softly, "your journey continues in India. You must find the Magic Carpet waiting for you there. Only the carpet can carry you safely across the desert winds and bring you back to the Moroccan sands." Behind her, the portal glowed brighter, revealing the Taj Mahal, lotus ponds, and elephants adorned in colours. The bears waved excitedly, urging Ari forward. The Guardian's voice wrapped around him like a blessing. "Go, little one. Retrieve the carpet. It will guide you back home."

The sun dipped low over Agra, casting golden light across the marble domes of the Taj Mahal. Ari stood hand-in-hand with Stinky, Smelly, and Sniffy, gazing at the monument's reflection in the still waters. Cherry blossom petals drifted around them like blessings from the sky. In the centre of the pool, a glowing lotus flower pulsed with quiet light a sign that this was not just a place, but a moment of awakening. The Taj Mahal, built from love and mourning, now stood as a symbol of eternal devotion and the promise that beauty can rise from sorrow. Ari felt it in his chest: this was where memory became strength, and where the journey turned inward toward truth.

The river glowed like liquid gold as Ari and his little companions stood on the ancient stone steps, watching the great lotus drift toward them with its flame burning bright at the centre. Hundreds of tiny candles floated across the water, each one carrying a wish, a prayer, or a memory released into the night. The air shimmered with warmth and quiet magic, as if the whole city was breathing in harmony with the river. Ari felt the stillness settle inside him a calm he hadn't known he needed. Here, on the sacred ghats of India, he understood that light is not only something you carry, but something you offer. And as the lotus flame flickered gently, he sensed that this place would teach him how to listen to the world with his heart.

Ari stepped closer to the floating carpet, eyes wide. “Guys… it’s really here, we found it” he whispered, his messy brown hair lifting in the magic breeze. Stinky bounced on his paws, his light-blue shirt wobbling. “Go on, Ari! Touch it! It’s been waiting for you!” Smelly twirled in her pink checkered skirt, giggling. “It’s so shiny! I think it likes you already!” Sniffy tugged at his green overalls and leaned forward. “Hurry, Ari! Once we have the carpet, we can fly all the way to the Moroccan desert!” Ari laughed softly, feeling braver with his friends beside him. “Alright,” he said, reaching out toward the shimmering threads of gold, “let’s go get our magic ride home.”

As the magic carpet soared above the shimmering river, Ari leaned forward, waving at the world below. "Look, guys! We're really flying!" he shouted, his voice bubbling with excitement. Stinky clung to the edge of the carpet, laughing. "I can see the whole city from up here!" Smelly twirled in place, her pink skirt fluttering in the wind. "The sky smells like flowers!" she giggled. Sniffy pointed toward the glowing domes and drifting hot-air balloons. "Ari, look! The Taj Mahal is sparkling like it's saying goodbye to us!" Ari grinned at his three brave friends. "Next stop… the Moroccan desert. Hold on tight adventure is waiting."

The magic carpet gave a sudden playful shake, almost like it was teasing them, and before Ari could grab the edge, it swooped upward with a soft flip! and drifted into the glowing sky. “Hey! Come back!” Ari laughed but gravity had other plans. He and the three bears tumbled gently into the warm sand, landing in a puff of golden dust. The moment they hit the dune, they began sliding faster, smoother, and more joyfully than they ever expected. The Moroccan Sahara carried them down its shimmering slope like a giant, sunlit slide. Ari stretched his arms wide, laughing as the wind rushed past his cheeks. Stinky spun beside him, Smelly squealed with delight, and Sniffy shouted, “This is even better than flying!” By the time they reached the bottom, breathless and glowing with excitement, the desert palace of Morocco rose before them waiting with ancient magic and the final gift of their journey.

The golden dunes shimmered as Ari stepped forward, the bears close behind, their eyes wide with wonder. The Guardian of Morocco stood tall in the sunset light, her veil glowing like starlight, her voice warm and steady. “I see you made it safely,” she said, smiling gently. “And you brought back the Magic Carpet that once belonged to us. It was taken long ago and never returned. Thank you, Ari, for bringing it home.”

The Moroccan Guardian reached out, and in her hands was a radiant star five points glowing softly, shaped like a perfect pentagram. “This is the Star of Wisdom,” she said. “It carries the memory of those who walked before you, and the courage to walk your own path. I want you to carry it now.” Ari cupped his hands, heart pounding, and received the star as if it were made of light itself. The bears leaned in, their faces lit by its glow, as the desert wind whispered, you are ready.

There it was nestled in the golden sand, glowing from within like a heartbeat the Septarian Egg. Smelly ran forward and wrapped her little arms around it, whispering, "We found it… we really found it." The cracked shell shimmered with light, and inside, a tiny dragon stirred, its silhouette flickering like a dream ready to wake. "There's a baby dragon in there," said Sniffy, eyes wide. "It's about to hatch!" Ari stepped closer, heart pounding, and looked up just in time to see the Guardian of Morocco begin to fade into the golden light. Her voice echoed softly, like wind through silk: "You've returned what was lost. The Magic Carpet… the Egg… and the truth of your heart." Ari blinked, unsure. "But what do we do now?" he asked. The desert was quiet, but the egg pulsed gently in Smelly's arms as if answering him without words.

The Septarian Egg glowed brighter and brighter until the cracks shimmered like tiny rivers of light. Then, with a soft ping! the shell burst open, and a swirl of golden sparkles filled the air. A tiny baby dragon tumbled out, blinking up at them with bright, curious eyes. Its wings fluttered like soft silk, and a joyful chirp escaped its little mouth. Ari gasped, jumping back in surprise, while the bears leapt into the air with excitement. Smelly clapped her paws, Stinky spun in circles, and Sniffy shouted, "He's here! The baby dragon is finally here!" The dragon wobbled on its feet, then looked straight at Ari as if it already knew him and a warm glow wrapped around them all, sealing the beginning of a brand-new bond.

The tiny dragon blinked up at them, glowing softly as if lit from the inside, and Ari suddenly understood why the Guardian had trusted them with this journey. This mystical creature wasn't just a baby dragon it was the Spirit of New Beginnings, born from courage, kindness, and the choices Ari made along the way. Its heartbeat carried the memory of every realm they had visited, every lesson they had learned. And the Septarian Crystal the ancient egg that had protected it represented unity, the way all the worlds were connected through wisdom, love, and truth. Its cracked patterns were like a map of Ari's own path: imperfect, brave, and full of light. As the dragon stretched its tiny wings, the crystal fragments shimmered around them, reminding Ari that even things that break can become the start of something magical.

The baby dragon stepped from the glowing shards of its Septarian shell and moved toward Ari with a soft, shimmering hum, as if recognizing him from a story written long before either of them were born. Golden light curled around them, warm and ancient, binding boy and dragon in a bond that felt older than the desert itself. When their hands finally touched Ari's small fingers meeting the dragon's glowing scales — a burst of light spiralled upward into the sky, painting the Sahara in ribbons of gold. Stinky, Smelly, and Sniffy watched in breathless awe as the desert wind whispered the truth: this was a moment that would be remembered for generations upon generations. The day a child and a dragon found each other, not by chance, but by destiny and the world quietly shifted toward a brighter future.

The moment Ari and the Septarian Dragon touched, a burst of pure white light spiralled into the sky, brighter than anything the desert had ever seen. The sand shimmered, the air hummed, and from the heart of that glowing beam, a swirling shape began to form. With a soft whoooosh, a Genie emerged tall, shimmering, and wrapped in robes of sapphire and gold. His eyes sparkled like ancient stars as he bowed deeply before Ari. "At last," he said with a warm smile, "the bond has been made. I am Azar, the Guardian Genie of Light. Your courage has awakened me from my long slumber." Ari blinked in awe as the Genie placed a hand over his heart. "Do not be afraid, young traveller. I have come to guide you, for your journey is far from over, it is time you go home."

The Genie's expression softened as the white dove circled above them, its wings scattering quiet light across the desert. "Ari," he said, his voice deep with ancient knowing, "every child who comes from your family carries a story, a strength, and sometimes a burden… but never alone." He placed the glowing memory-gift into Ari's hands, warm as a heartbeat. "This is your reminder and Papou Costa's that love never disappears. It simply changes shape, passing from one generation to the next, just as your family legacy now lives through you." Ari held the light close, feeling it settles into him like a promise, something he would carry forward long after this moment faded into legend.

The Genie stepped closer, his robes shimmering like the last colours of sunset, and placed his glowing hand gently over Ari's heart. "You have travelled far, little one," he said, his voice soft as drifting sand. "And you have carried courage, kindness, and truth in every step." A warm light flowed from his palm into Ari's chest, not heavy like magic, but gentle like a blessing meant to last a lifetime. The bears watched in stillness as the Genie continued, "Wherever you go, this light will guide you. It will remind you of who you are, and of all those who walked beside you." Behind him, the baby dragon fluttered its wings, and the white dove circled above as if sealing the moment. The Genie smiled, a knowing, timeless smile. "Go forward with peace, Ari. The worlds you touched will never forget you… and neither will I."

The Genie's blessing still glowed warmly in Ari's chest as the world around him began to soften, as though the edges of the desert were turning to mist. The white dove circled above, its wings scattering tiny sparks that drifted down like falling stars. The baby dragon curled close to him, humming a lullaby only ancient creatures knew, and the three bears floated gently beside him as if held by an invisible breeze. The Genie placed a steady hand on Ari's shoulder, his smile full of kindness and something deeper  a knowing. "Wherever you go next," he said softly, "this light will stay with you. It will guide you home, and it will guide you forward." The colors of the sky shimmered, growing softer, warmer, almost like the glow of a familiar room. Ari felt himself growing lighter, as though the magic was carrying him somewhere safe. The Genie's voice drifted with him, gentle as a whisper. "Rest now, little traveler. Your journey continues in ways you have yet to see."

Ari's eyes fluttered open to a warm, golden glow, the kind that felt strangely familiar, as though it had followed him from somewhere far away. For a moment he lay still, the soft hum of the baby dragon's warmth still lingering in his chest, the echo of the Genie's blessing drifting through his mind like a fading melody. Stinky, Smelly, and Sniffy were tucked beside him exactly where he had left them, yet somehow they felt closer, as if they had travelled with him through every moment of the night. The room was quiet except for the gentle morning light slipping through the curtains, carrying the faint scent of something sweet, chocolate, maybe, and the distant sound of his mum moving in the kitchen. Ari stretched, a small smile forming as he whispered to himself, "It felt so real…" And as he sat up, the world outside seemed brighter, softer, touched by the same magic he had just lived. It was Easter Sunday and somehow, he felt different, as though he had brought a piece of the dream back with him.

Ari burst out of his room with the same excitement that had carried him through deserts and stars only moments before. His little feet pattered across the hallway as he raced toward the kitchen, the soft echo of the Genie's blessing still warming his chest. The morning sunlight spilled across the tiles like golden magic, and there waiting on the table was the Easter hamper, overflowing with colourful eggs, a soft bunny, and a golden surprise that shimmered just enough to make his heart skip. His puppy and kitten scampered beside him, as if they too felt the leftover sparkle of the night's adventure. Mummy stood by the counter in her rainbow robe, smiling over her mug as Ari skidded to a stop, eyes wide with wonder. For a moment, he wasn't sure if he was still dreaming… because somehow, the magic felt as though it had followed him home.

Ari reached into the basket with small, curious hands, expecting the cool smoothness of a chocolate egg but instead, his fingers brushed something warm, almost alive. He lifted the Septarian Egg slowly, its golden glow pulsing faintly against his palms, and for a breathless moment the whole kitchen seemed to fall silent. Ari's eyes softened, filling with a feeling he didn't have words for something between wonder and longing, something that felt like love reaching across worlds. He held the egg close, and in that instant he felt Papou Costa… not as a memory, not as a story, but as a presence, gentle and proud, standing right beside him. It was only a moment, but it wrapped around Ari like a hug from someone he missed more than he understood. And he knew without knowing how that this egg wasn't just a dream following him home. It was a reminder that the people we love never truly leave us. They simply find new ways to stay.

**DEDICATION**

**To Papou Costa,** whose love, wisdom, and quiet strength continue to guide me every step of the way. Your light lives in our stories, in our traditions, and in the hearts of the children who carry your name forward.

**To Yia-Yia Dimi,** whose hands shaped our traditions, whose stories carried our history, and whose love continues to guide us long after the candles burn low. Your strength, your faith, and your gentle wisdom keeping our family traditions from losing their lustre live on in Ari, and in every generation that follows.

**To Ari,** the little boy who reminds me how lucky I am to have him. When times are tough, you still bring me hope. I know you are still learning, and I can be impatient sometimes but I'm learning too. For courage begins with kindness, and kindness is not always easy in a world that can be cruel. The magic we pass from one generation to the next is the greatest legacy of all.

To every Family, past, present, and still to come may you always feel the warmth of those who came before you and may love to be the thread that binds your stories together.

**Panagiota Makaronis; Author**

**Moral to the Story**

The world is made of many cultures, many faiths, and many paths yet at the heart of every tradition lies the same truth: we are all human, and we all deserve to be treated with dignity and respect. No racism. No insults. No division.

Just the reminder that every belief system carries its own beauty, and every person carries their own light. Humanity has travelled, migrated, learned, and evolved for thousands of years. Stories have been told, scriptures written, manuscripts preserved each one a reflection of people searching for meaning, hope, and connection.

Though the words may differ, the message is shared: choose kindness, seek peace, and honour the humanity in one another. There is no need for discrimination. No need for war. Peace is not a dream it is a choice we make every day.

We are born the same way, and we leave this world the same way. Whatever we gather in this life wealth, possessions, achievements stay behind. What remains is how we treated others, how we loved, and how we lived, and yet, life is not always gentle.

There have been moments where hurt has worn me down, where kindness felt like something I gave even when no one offered it back. People are not always what they seem faces can be false, promises can be empty, intentions can be misleading.

I learned to hide parts of myself just to find a little peace, building quiet walls around my heart not out of anger, but out of survival. From behind those walls, I saw something clearly: many people have forgotten their own value, their own spirit, their sense of unity.

And in a world where worth is measured by what you can offer, asking for help can leave you feeling smaller than before sometimes wishing you had never asked at all. But even this truth carries a lesson: humanity is not finished when things go wrong.

We are all learning, all stumbling, all trying to find our way. Some mistakes are accidents, and some are intentional designed to turn a victim into a villain. But the story does not end there. Because nothing stays the same forever. People change, because Stories change.

Overall, I would Love to believe that peace can still be chosen, regardless. In the end, we are here for a shared purpose: to live with compassion, to walk with humility, and to build a world where peace is stronger than fear, and unity is stronger than the walls we hide behind.

**AMEN**

**Χριστός Ανέστη**

**Happy Easter to all**

*May the light of the Resurrection fill your homes, your hearts, and every story yet to be told.*

**AMEN**

Ari's Adventure:
Journey of Magic and Wonder
Australia
The Beginning
Dragon Egg Crystal
Greece
Wisdom & Light
Feather of Athena, Staff of Hermes
Italy
Courage & Unity
Golden Key of Courage
Jerusalem
Sacred & Holy
Cross of Light
Egypt
Ancient Knowledge
Ankh of Life
India
Colour & Magic
Lotus of Light, Magic Carpet
China
Harmony & Dragons
Dragon Pearl of Harmony
Morocco
Desert & Destiny
Final Destination
Dragon Egg Crystal
Sniffy
Smelly
Stinky
N
E
S
W

www.ingramcontent.com/pod-product-compliance
Lightning Source LLC
LaVergne TN
LVHW052254100826
845147LV00001B/41

* 9 7 8 1 7 6 4 4 5 8 1 4 6 *